A Very Vegan Halloween

A Very Vegan Halloween

The Witch's Cauldron Cookbook

REBECCA HENRY

Food photography prepared and taken by Rebecca Henry using clip2comic software.

Cover Design by Rebecca Henry using stock image: ID 125021650© Rimma Bondarenko | Dreamstime.com

Stock Images:

ID 100670994© 9dreamstudio | Dreamstime.com

ID 132173263© NatashaBreen | Dreamstime.com

ID 155607040© Amberto4ka | Dreamstime.com

ID 127863785© Amberto4ka | Dreamstime.com

ID 61177851© Vitalii Shastun | Dreamstime.com

ID 101275678© Rimma Bondarenko | Dreamstime.com

ID 99588054© Zmiter | Dreamstime.com

ID 44111051© Stockcreations | Dreamstime.com

ID 123925285© Santusya | Dreamstime.com

Contents

Recipe Disclaimer

Cooking and baking is so much fun, but it is also extremely subjective. No two people will come out with the exact same result even when using the same recipe. Just like any art form or craft individuality makes the project your own! The images used in this book are to inspire and ignite your imagination while preparing the recipes. Make sure you, nor the person you are preparing the food for, are allergic to any of the ingredients. Before beginning, gather all the necessary tools and use the appropriate measurements in each recipe. Also, remember when cooking the food, that our ovens might have different temperatures, or you and I might use different brands of the same ingredients, or you might decide to use almond extract instead of vanilla extract. All these little differences could affect the outcome of the recipe. Try not to worry about what your level of cooking and baking abilities might be. Cooking and baking is like everything else in the artistic world, the more you do it the better you will become. My advice is to try all the recipes that appeal to you and have fun with them! A little tip when trying a new recipe is to read and re-read the recipe, feel comfortable with it before you begin! And if you've never tried vegan cooking before, please keep in mind some nondairy recipes will have different textures than what you might be used to with dairy. Happy cooking and baking and most importantly have A Very Vegan Halloween!

Conversions

All the measurements in this book are based on the imperial system. Oven temperatures are in Fahrenheit.

Abbreviations Used In This Cookbook:

- tsp – teaspoon
- tbsp. – tablespoon
- lbs. – pounds
- oz – ounces

Fahrenheit to Celsius conversion

Fahrenheit	Celsius
325 degrees F	165 degrees C
350 degrees F	177 degrees C
375 degrees F	190 degrees C
400 degrees F	200 degrees C
425 degrees F	220 degrees C

Cups To Grams Conversion:

Nondairy butter to grams

- 1 cup = 230 grams
- 3/4 cup = 173 grams
- 2/3 cup = 153 grams

- 1/2 cup = 115 grams
- 1/3 cup = 77 grams
- 1/4 cup = 58 grams

All-purposed flour

- 1 cup = 125 grams
- ¾ cup = 94 grams
- 2/3 cup = 83 grams
- 1/2 cup = 63 grams
- 1/3 cup = 42 grams
- 1/4 cup = 31 grams

Oils to grams

- 1 cup = 225 grams
- 3/4 cup = 170 grams
- 2/3 cup = 150 grams
- 1/2 cup = 113 grams
- 1/3 cup = 75 grams
- 1/4 cup = 56 grams

Liquid to milliliters

- 1 cup = 240 ml
- 3/4 cup = 190 ml
- 2/3 cup = 170 ml
- 1/2 cup = 125 ml
- 1/3 cup = 80 ml
- 1/4 cup = 60 ml

Sugar

- 1 cup = 200 grams
- 3/4 cup = 150 grams
- 2/3 cup = 133 grams
- 1/2 cup = 100 grams
- 1/3 cup = 67 grams

- 1/4 cup = 50 grams

Powdered sugar

- 1 cup = 125 grams
- 3/4 cup = 94 grams
- 2/3 cup = 83 grams
- 1/2 cup = 63 grams
- 1/3 cup = 42 grams
- 1/4 cup = 31 grams

kitchen Witch Essentials

- Spatula
- Rolling pin
- Pizza Cutter
- Measuring cup
- Measuring spoons
- Wire rack
- Cookie sheet
- Parchment paper
- Whisker
- Food Processor
- Stand Mixer
- Baking Pan
- Colander
- Frying Pan
- Pastry Bag

I use a *Kitchen Aid* stand mixer and *Black and Decker* food processor for preparing my recipes. I am not sponsored by either company.

Ingredients

All ingredients in the recipes are vegan and I use a wide array of products when cooking. I'm American, but I am currently living in the UK. My brand choices have changed according to my surroundings and available options, but most countries do offer vegan brands. It truly comes down to personal preference and what is available in your area. I also try to purchase organic ingredients when possible. Below is a list of some main ingredient options you can use from the provided recipes. I have not been sponsored by any of these brands listed below.

- **Butter:** *Earth Balance* is my go-to choice. They are organic as well.
- **Milk:** I prefer oat milk but almond and soy work the same.
- **Egg Replacer:** I use egg replacer powder (*Bob's Red Mill*) any brand or type will do.
- **Flour:** All-purpose organic unbleached white flour.
- **Sugar:** Organic white sugar or organic brown sugar. (cane sugar has animal bone char)
- **Nondairy Chocolate:** Vegan chocolate chips and baking chunks are available. *Enjoy Life* is an excellent brand, it is also a fair trade brand.
- **Vegan Sausages:** *Quorn* sausages and *Beyond Meat* sausages are my favorites. (any type of vegan soy dog will work as well)
- **Marshmallows:** *Freedom Marshmallows* are vegan.
- **Nondairy White Chocolate Baking Coins:** *King David Easy Melt White Baking Chocolate Coins* are the ones I like to use for taste and melting quality.
- **Mozzarella Nondairy Cheese Log:** *Mozza-Risella Log* Cheese
- **Sliced Nondairy Cheddar Cheese:** *Free From* and *Follow Your Heart* are the two brands I use.
- **Nondairy Cool Whip:** *So Delicious* Dairy Free.

Contents

- Revolting Meatless Meatball
- Gruesome Goblin Fettuccini with Specter Pasta Sauce
- Wicked Easy Webbed Pizza
- Menacing Monster Sweet Potato Burgers

DESSERTS

- Trick Or Treat Jelly
- Shockingly Simple Sugar Cookies
- Under Your Spell Witch Fingers
- Frightening Frosting
- Cursed Pumpkin Frosting
- Morbid Marshmallow Syrup
- Screaming Pumpkins Sugar Cookies
- Banshee Pumpkin Cupcakes With Wicked Witch Raspberry Syrup
- Going Batty Chocolate Cupcakes
- Eerie Edible Eyeballs
- Wicked Witch Raspberry Syrup
- Vampire Vanilla ice cream
- Spooky Spirit Cake Squares with Morbid Marshmallow Syrup
- Skele-cakes With White Chocolate Pretzels
- Bewitching Autumn Apples
- Chronically Confused Chocolate Chip Cookies
- Spell Binding Candy Apples

DRINKS

- Witches' Brew Hot Chocolate
- Wild Wizard Potion
- Zombie Party Punch
- Hobgoblin Pumpkin Punch

Introduction

I love Halloween! Wait that me rephrase that...I AM OBSESSED WITH HALLOWEEN! It is my absolute favorite holiday, and every year I dress up as a witch. Being a mom of two kids, I became even more obsessed with the spirit of this magical season. I live to throw Halloween bashes, decked out with decorations, party games, pinatas, spooky gift bags, but most importantly FOOD! Lots and lots and lots of Halloween food! Your eyes are the gateway to your stomach and presentation with spooky, fun food truly makes a party! It is imperative to me that my guests love the dishes I serve. I want them to enjoy every mouthful of tantalizing goodness they receive on their plates. I not only want the presentation to be engaging, but I need the taste to back up the visual appeal. The purpose of this book is to inspire your Halloween season by introducing basic but, tasty recipes that you can jazz up with Halloween flare galore! I'll be providing vegan dishes with options to add on and make your own. My intention is to show you lots of different alternatives to meat and dairy favorite meals, with a vegan option both kids and adults will love! Some of the biggest responses I get for going vegan are "I can't give up food!" or "What would I eat?!"

Lots of people believe they won't be able to reproduce traditional holiday recipes with vegan options. My goal is to show you can still throw a killer Halloween party, and wow all your guests with tasty and clever dishes. Kids love anything with eyes, spiders, or worms. I'll introduce some toppings that make little monsters want to gobble up their plates! Whether you are throwing a Halloween bash or just looking to have fun in the kitchen with your tiny ghouls, goblins, princesses, and knights, this book is sure to inspire Halloween fun for everyone!

Much love! Rebecca Henry

The Kitchen Witch

The kitchen is the heart and hearth of all homes. It is the place families gather and company is always welcomed. Children connect the kitchen as a place of safety and magic. The tantalizing aromas of home-baked goods hovering from the oven, filling the home with comfort and security, is a childhood memory I find most dear to me. Saturday morning pancakes with delicious maple syrup and fresh berries still tickle my senses with joy from my childhood to this day. Now I am the one preparing meals and filling my family and friend's bellies with comfort and love.

When you prepare a meal from scratch, using basic ingredients you are creating magic in your home. Every dish you prepare is infused with love, goodwill, and the intent for your family and friends to feel happy and loved. Kitchen Witches, also known as cottage witches, believe there is an opportunity for everyday, practical magic in the kitchen. With each meal the kitchen witch prepares, she is sending love, light, and good intentions to her loved ones.

Traits Of A Kitchen Witch

- She will leave charm bags around the home to bring good luck, prosperity, and abundance.
- You might find her in the garden at night, barefoot in the moonlight, burying a blessing bottle under a lavender plant to ensure happiness

and prosperity to her home.

- She always enchants the herbs cut fresh from her garden, before sprinkling them into her recipes, whispering silently to herself.
- You will find salt sprinkled in her doorway to ward off negativity.
- She will make lavender sachets and place them under your pillow to bring tranquility and a peaceful night's sleep.
- She will make a poultice from coconut oil & herbs to heal cuts and burns.
- She will have a witch cabinet in the heart of her home stocked with dried herbs, oils, premade tonics, and crystals.
- You will find her blowing loose eyelashes off your finger, guiding you to make a wish and saying it twice.
- She never wears shoes in the garden, her bare feet will always be grounded in the earth.
- She throws salt over her shoulder whenever it is spilled, smiling secretly to herself.
- Her black cat always accompanies her in the kitchen, coming and going through the open window overlooking her vegetable patch.
- She will carry a crystal in her pocket tied with twine and a lock of her lover's hair for luck.
- Her kitchen is always open to those who need a moment of guidance accompanied by a cup of tea. If you look closely inside the empty teacup you might see your future husband's name written in the leaves.

You too can be a kitchen witch with a few ingredients, positive thoughts, and love.

1. Snacks

- Bare Boned Breadsticks
- Cackle Cauldron Witch Fingers
- Mysteriously Dreadful Mummy Sausages
- Spectacular Specter Sauce
- Horribly Horrifying Black Bean Hummus
- Ghastly Grim Basil Pesto
- Hocus Pocus Jack-O'-Lanterns (Bell Peppers with Veggies)
- Nice and toasty pizza webs
- Boo-tiful Boo Bananas
- Perfect Party Cutie Pumpkins
- Creepy Crawly Skinless Spiders
- Grinning Granny Apples
- Enchanted Eyeball Logs

PART I

BARE BONES BREADSTICKS

Prep Time: 40 mins / Cook Time: 10-15 mins / Servings: Makes approx. 10

Ingredients

- 3 ½-4 cups all-purpose flour
- 1 tbsp. instant yeast
- 1 tbsp. sugar
- 1 tsp. salt
- 1 ½ cups warm water
- ¼ cup non-dairy butter (for greasing the pan and coating the bones)

Instructions

1. Preheat oven to 400 degrees Fahrenheit.
2. In a mixing bowl dissolve the yeast into warm water. Allow a few minutes for the yeast to activate.
3. Using a stand mixer with a bread dough attachment, combine flour, sugar, and salt (or mix well by hand).

4. Add the yeast mixture to the flour mixture and stir together.
5. Knead for 3 minutes on slow speed in a stand mixture then let it rest for 10 minutes covered with a kitchen towel. If you are mixing by hand knead for 10 minutes.
6. Melt the non-dairy butter and spread half of the non-dairy butter onto a baking sheet.
7. Lightly sprinkle some flour onto your work surface and roll out the dough. Work the dough into a rectangle about the same size as your baking sheet.
8. Use a pizza cutter to cut the dough into one-inch-wide strips. Split each end of the dough strips to about 1 inch on both sides of each piece. These will be the ends of the bones.
9. Roll and curl each end piece outward to give the breadstick a captivating bone look. (Don't worry about it looking perfect, bones are supposed to look odd and quirky so have fun with this!)
10. Place each breadstick on the buttered baking sheet and brush the tops of the breadsticks with the remaining melted non-dairy butter. The more nondairy butter the better right?!
11. Optional step – sprinkle each bone with garlic salt.
12. Let the bones rise for about 10 minutes before baking.
13. Bake for about 10-15 minutes, until the edges begin to turn golden brown.
14. Once cooled, chow down on these drooling temptations and serve with your choice of devilish dipping sauce.

Witches' Notes: See recipe index for sauce and dip options.

PART II
CACKLE CAULDRON WITCH FINGERS

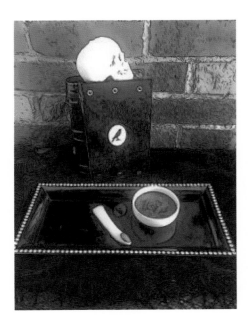

Prep Time: 40 mins / Cook Time: 10-12 mins / Servings: Makes approx. 10

Ingredients

- 3 ½ cups all-purpose flour
- 1 ½ cups of non-dairy milk (I use oat milk)
- 1 tsp. baking powder
- ½ tsp. salt
- 2 tbsp. sugar
- ¼ cup non-dairy butter (for greasing the pan and topping off the witch fingers)
- almonds

Instructions

1. Preheat oven to 400 degrees Ferineheight.
2. In a mixing bowl mix flour, salt, sugar, and baking powder.
3. Using a stand mixer with a bread dough attachment, slowly start to add the non-dairy milk to the mixture. Mix on slow speed (or mix by hand well). Like a witch with her cauldron, slow and steady produces the best results. Mix until the dough becomes smooth and elastic. If the dough is too sticky add more flour, 1 tbsp. at a time until you can form it into a ball. If it is too dry add non-dairy milk, 1 tbsp. at a time until it reaches the right doughy consistency. If mixing by hand knead the dough for 10 minutes.
4. Let the dough rise for 10 minutes in a bowl covered with a kitchen towel.
5. Melt the non-dairy butter and spread half onto a baking sheet.
6. Roll the dough on a lightly floured working surface into a rectangle about the same size as the baking sheet. Don't roll your dough too thin. You don't want the fingers to break when you move them to your baking sheet. If they are too thin, this will make the witch fingers hard to manage. If this happens, regather your dough, form another ball and reroll the dough thicker, and begin again.
7. Using a pizza cutter, cut the dough into 1″ wide x 4″ long strips. Place the fingers on your baking sheet.
8. Press almonds in one end of the breadsticks for the fingernails.
9. Lightly score each knuckle with a sharp knife. This gives the fingers dimension and texture.
10. Coat each finger well with the remaining non-dairy butter.
11. Optional step to sprinkle garlic powder or sea salt on each finger. Do you want your witch fingers to be garlicky or salty? The choice is yours.
12. Let the fingers rise for 10 minutes on the baking sheet.
13. Bake for about 10-12 minutes, until the edges begin to turn golden brown. I always check at the earliest time when trying a new recipe. Like I mentioned previously, oven temperatures can vary. Play it safe on your first try and peek on these beauties at 10 minutes.
14. Serve these creepy delicacies with your choice of intoxicating dipping sauces.

Witch's Notes: See recipe index for sauce and dip options.

Witch's Comments: If you lay out your presentation with extra touches using props, you kick up the wow factor! When creating a spread for a party, use props to bring your dishes to life. Recipes have personalities just like the baker who prepares them. What personality do you want your dish to have? A simple prop like a chalkboard with the words; "Happy Halloween" or "Trick or Treat" or even "Stop in for a Spell" in the center of your witch fingers adds a visual appeal. Get creative! If you have a cauldron use it for the dipping sauce. Halloween is all about fun and Cackle Cauldron Witch Fingers screams fun at a party!

PART III

MYSTERIOUSLY DREADFUL MUMMY SAUSAGES

Prep Time: about 3 hours / Cook Time: 10-15 mins / Servings: Makes approx. 6-8

Ingredients

2 packets of Quorn Sausages

Croissant Dough

- 2 ¼ tsp. active yeast
- ¼ cup warm water
- 3-4 cups all-purpose flour white
- 1 tsp. salt
- 1 ¼ cup oat milk (any non-dairy milk will work)
- ¼ cup walnut oil
- 3 tbsp. sugar
- 1 tbsp. olive oil (for coating the bowl)
- ¼ cup non-dairy butter (for greasing the pan and topping off the mummies)

Instructions

- 1. Preheat oven to 375 degrees Fahrenheit.
  2. In a mixing bowl, mix warm water and yeast. Let is sit for a couple of minutes to activate the yeast. Make sure the water is warm, not hot.
  3. In a stand mixer combine all the wet ingredients, including the yeast and water. Mix on slow speed for one minute using a bread dough attachment (or mix well by hand).
  4. Add all dry ingredients and slowly add 3 cups of flour. If the dough appears very wet slowly add in the remaining cup of flour. The aim is for the dough to feel slightly sticky. If the dough is too sticky add an extra tablespoon of flour if needed. If it becomes too dry add 1 tbsp. of water at a time until the desired consistency is reached.
  5. Knead on slow speed until the dough is smooth and elastic (or knead by hand for 10 minutes).
  6. Coat a medium-large bowl with olive oil, and transfer the dough, making sure to rub the dough in the oiled bowl, covering the top and bottom of the dough ball.
  7. Cover with a kitchen towel and allow to rise 1-2 hours, until the dough has doubled in size.
  8. Roll your dough out into a large rectangle on a lightly floured surface, about the size of your baking sheet.
  9. Using a pizza cutter, cut the dough into thin strips. This doesn't have to be an exact size. The size of the strips all depends on the look you want for your mummy dogs. The thinner the strip the more wraps you will have.
  10. Time to dress your dogs! Wrap your dogs in the strips of dough so they look like strips of cloth on a mummy.
  11. Grease your baking sheet with half of the melted non-dairy butter and lay your mummies on top. Brush the tops of your mummies with the remaining non-dairy butter. Optional step, sprinkle sea salt or garlic salt on top of each mummy.
  12. Bake for about 10-15 mins, or until the dough is a golden brown. You don't want to overcook these so keep your eye on them and check these dreadful mummies at 10 mins exactly.
  13. Add dobs of mustard for eyes or edible eyeballs and serve with your favorite dipping sauce that will make anyone drool with enjoyment.

Witch's Notes: See recipe index for sauce and dip options as well as the recipe for Eerie Edible Eyeballs.

Witch's Comments: This is a brilliant recipe project you can do with little ones. At one of my daughter's Halloween parties, I had all the guests wrap up their own mummy dogs. To make life easier I premade the dough before the party. I set up stations with different recipes and had all the guests prepare some of the food. Not only did they have fun wrapping up their dogs, but they also enjoyed eating the food! None of the girls were vegan so this was a wonderful opportunity to see them enjoy a plant-based, cruelty-free food item that they had never had before, and they truly enjoyed it! Some of the girls had their parents buy vegan dogs after making the mummy wraps.

PART IV

SPECTACULAR SPECTER SAUCE

Prep Time: 10 mins / Cook Time: 15-20 mins / Servings: Approx. 4 people

Ingredients

- 1 large can crushed tomatoes (28 ounces)
- 1 yellow onion (finely chopped)
- 2 cloves garlic (minced)
- 1 tbsp. extra virgin olive oil
- 1 tsp. dried oregano
- 1 tbsp. Italian seasoning blend
- 1 tsp. basil
- 1 tsp. salt
- 2 tbsp. white sugar (optional)

Instructions

1. In a saucepan warm 1 tbsp. of olive oil over medium-high heat. Add the onions and sauté until softened and translucent, about 2 minutes. Next, add garlic and cook for another minute.
2. Add the tomatoes (including juices from the tin), salt, and all the spices to the saucepan and stir well.
3. Bring the sauce to a simmer over medium-high heat then reduce the temperature and simmer for 10 minutes.
4. Remove from heat and use over pasta, pizza, or breadsticks.

Witch's Notes: If you like your sauce sweet you can add up to ¼ cup of sugar. In my personal opinion 1-2 tbsp. should suffice however, I've had guests who love their sauce sweet. This is your recipe you decide what tastes good to your taste buds. Like the witch in the forest with Hansel and Gretel sweeter may be better for some.

PART V

HORRIBLY HORRIFYING BLACK BEAN HUMMUS

Prep Time: 5 mins / Cook Time: 10 mins / Servings: Approx. 4-6 people

Ingredients

- 2 x 15oz cans of black beans drained and rinsed.
- 2 cloves garlic
- 2 tbsp. tahini
- 3 tbsp. lime juice
- ½ tsp. salt
- black olives

For design: non-dairy sour cream

Instructions

1. In a food processor add the garlic cloves and process until finely chopped.
2. Next, add the drained and rinsed black beans and mix until pureed. It should be a lovely shade of black.
3. Add all remaining ingredients and process until smooth and creamy.
4. Spoon the hummus into a dip bowl. I like to use a white bowl to contrast with the black color of the hummus.
5. Fill a pastry bag with nondairy sour cream and pipe your most spine-chilling spider web onto the hummus. Top with a black olive spider and serve with fresh vegetables or Mysteriously Dreadful Mummy Sausages, Bare Boned Breadsticks, or Cackle Cauldron Witch Fingers.

Witch's Notes: To make the spider, place one black olive as the body on your hummus and slice up 1-2 more black olives using the pieces as legs. Position the sliced legs on either side of the whole black olive.

PART VI
GHASTLY GRIM BASIL PESTO

Prep Time: 1-2 mins / Cook Time: 5 mins / Servings: Approx. 4-6 people

Ingredients

- ¼ cup pine nuts
- ¼ cup extra virgin olive oil
- 2 cups basil leaves
- 1 tsp. minced garlic
- 1 tbsp. lemon juice
- ¼ cup warm water
- ½ tsp. sea salt

Instructions

1. Add all the ingredients into a food processor and process on high until

well combined. If you want the pesto smoother and thinner, slowly add more water to the pesto 1 tbsp. at a time until you reach your desired consistency.

2. Scoop the pesto into dip bowls and serve with Mysteriously Dreadful Mummy Sausages, Bare Boned Breadsticks, or Cackle Cauldron Witch Fingers. You can also use the pesto sauce to turn pasta into a gruesome green.

PART VII

HOCUS POCUS JACK-O'-LANTERNS

Prep Time: 5 mins / Cook Time: 10 mins / Servings: Makes approx. 4

Ingredients

- yellow, red and orange bell peppers (washed)
- sliced vegetables of your choice or lettuce
- cooked spaghetti (optional replacement instead of veggies)

Instructions

1. Wash and prep all the vegetables and let dry.
2. Cut off the top of each pepper. Remove and discard all the cores and seeds.
3. Using a sharp paring knife, carve a fun Jack-O'-Lantern face into each pepper. If you feel uncertain about carving the face, trace an outline first on each bell pepper using an edible marker. Be creative here and mix up the faces. The more personality these peppers have the better. We are going for personal peppers with personality! Try saying that ten times fast as you carve.
4. Position the peppers upright on a ghoulish serving dish. Fill each bell pepper with your choice of sliced vegetables or make a personal-sized

salad.

5. Serve these morbid delights with your favorite hummus or dressing. See index for recipe options.

Witch's Notes: You can also fill the peppers with cooked spaghetti, having the noodles ooze out of the carved mouth, nose, and eyes.

PART VIII

NICE AND TOASTY PIZZA WEB

Prep Time: 5 mins / Cook Time: 5-10 mins / Servings: Makes approx. 6 Snowman Pancakes

Ingredients

- organic sliced bread of your choice
- tomato sauce
- non-dairy mozzarella cheese (I use almond mozzarella cheese)
- non-dairy butter
- black olives (optional step to make edible spiders)

Instructions

1. Preheat the oven to 350 degrees Fahrenheit.
2. Butter the underside of each bread slice and place on a baking sheet.
3. Spread a thin layer of tomato sauce over the top of the bread.
4. Top with non-dairy cheese and create a web-like pattern. Remember

webs aren't perfect so don't stress about making them completely accurate. This is about having fun with the food.

5. Bake for 5-10 mins or until the cheese has lightly melted. You don't want to overcook these spidery devils.

6. Top with fun edible spiders to give it a creepy Halloween vibe and watch your guests get caught up in these delicious webs!

Witch's Notes: Optional step to add edible spiders to the pizza by using black olives. Place one black olive as the body on your pizza and slice up 2 more black olives using the pieces as legs. Position the sliced legs on either side of the whole black olive. Such spidery fun!

PART IX

BOO-TIFUL BOO BANANAS

Prep Time: 1-2 mins / Cook Time: 5 mins / Servings: Makes approx. 4

Ingredients

- bananas 2-3
- non-dairy mini chocolate chips

Instructions

1. Peel the bananas and cut them in half. Discard the peels.
2. Press the mini non-dairy chocolate chips inside the bananas for eyes. Do you feel like someone is looking at you?
3. Place each banana upright on a ghostly serving tray and get ready to spook your guests! BOO!

Witch's Comments: This may seem like a simple recipe, but the wow factor it receives at a party is unbelievable! Boo-tiful Boo Bananas not only look amazing as a standalone side dish, but they are also the perfect prop to use for other dishes. These bananas are too boo-tiful to be left on their own, incorporate them with other dishes and see how pleasantly surprised you'll be with the results! This makes a great school treat for classrooms. Pair the

Boo-tiful Boo Bananas with Perfect Party Cutie Pumpkins. Teachers and kids alike will love them!

PART X

PERFECT PARTY CUTIE PUMPKINS

Prep Time: 5 mins / Cook Time: 5 mins / Servings: Makes approx. 6

Ingredients

- cuties (tangerines or mandarins work as well)
- 1 stalk celery

Instructions

1. Peel the cuties and discard the skins.
2. Wash and dry the celery. Slice and cut the celery into small thin sticks. You don't want them big. Small and steady wins this race.
3. Stick the celery sticks into the tops of the cuties to create an adorable pumpkin stem.
4. Arrange your pumpkins on a decorative serving tray and watch your guest coo over these cuties!

Witch's Notes: Add these cuties to your boo-tiful boo bananas and create a spread your guests won't be able to keep their hands off!

PART XI

CREEPY CRAWLY SKINLESS SPIDER

Prep Time: 5 mins / Cook Time: 5-10 mins / Servings: Makes approx. 2

Ingredients

- 1 bag of tangerines (3 tangerines make 1 spider)
- non-dairy candy eyeballs (see Eerie Edible Eyeballs recipe for homemade)

Instructions

1. Skin one whole tangerine and lay it upright on your serving tray.
2. Skin another tangerine slightly smaller than the first. Sizes vary so sort out one slightly smaller and position it in front of the larger one to make a head on your serving tray.
3. Skin another tangerine and divide the pieces into 8 sections to make the legs. Position 4 pieces on one side of the body and the remaining 4 on the other side.
4. Add non-dairy candy eyeballs to give your Creepy Crawly Skinless Spider a contagious face that anyone would want to gobble up!

Witch's Notes: See Eerie Edible Eyeball recipe for homemade eyeballs.

PART XII

GRINNING GRANNY APPLE

Prep Time: 5 mins / Cook Time: 5-10 mins / Servings: Makes approx. 4

Ingredients

- 4 granny smith apples (any type of apple will work)
- peanut butter (you can use almond butter as well)
- non-dairy mini marshmallows (or cashew nuts)
- non-dairy eyeballs (see Eerie Edible Eyeballs recipe for homemade)

Instructions

1. Use a paring knife to cut the middles of quartered apples to create smiley-looking mouths.
2. Generously spread the mouths with peanut butter. I go heavy on the peanut butter, but you can add as much or as little as you like.
3. Place non-dairy mini marshmallows into the apples to create teeth. Crooked teeth are spooky and appropriate for Halloween, so don't

worry about perfection.

4. Use peanut butter to "glue" each eye above the mouths.
5. Place on your best serving tray. Look at these grinning granny goblins' smiles!

Witch's Comments: The first time I prepared these they were gone in minutes. Kids absolutely love the funny appeal and look of these apples.

PART XIII

ENCHANTED EYEBALL LOG

Prep Time: 5 mins / Cook Time: 5-10 mins / Servings: Makes approx. 5

Ingredients

- 5 stalks of celery (cut into halves)
- 10 tbsp. peanut butter
- non-dairy edible eyeballs (Eerie Edible Eyeballs for homemade)

Instructions

1. Wash and dry your celery stalks. Cut into halves.
2. Place peanut butter into a pastry bag and pipe out your peanut butter on each celery stalk.
3. Top with edible eyeballs (see Eerie Edible Eyeball recipe in index).
4. Serve on a platter alone or with Creepy Crawley Skinless Spiders,

Bootiful Boo Bananas, Grinning Granny Apple Goblins, and Perfect Party Cutie Pumpkins to make a serving platter your guest are sure to talk about!

2. Mains

- Pumpkin Cobweb Pancakes
- Haunted Spiced Oatmeal
- Perfectly Petrifying Pumpkin Soup
- Poltergeist Party Mashed Potatoes
- Revolting Meatless Meatball
- Gruesome Goblin Fettuccini with Specter Pasta Sauce
- Wicked Easy Webbed Pizza
- Menacing Monster Sweet Potato Burgers

PART XIV

PUMPKIN COBWEB PANCAKES

Prep Time: 10 mins / Cook Time: 20-30 mins / Servings: Makes approx.   6

Ingredients

- 2 ¼ cups all-purpose flour
- 2 tsp. baking powder
- ¼ cup sugar
- ¼ cup brown sugar
- ½ tsp. cinnamon
- 1 tsp. pumpkin pie spice
- 1 1/2 cup oat milk (any non-dairy milk will work)
- 2 tsp. lemon juice
- 1/2 cup water
- 1/2 cup pumpkin puree
- 1 tsp. vanilla extract
- pinch of salt

- coconut oil or coconut cooking spray
- non-dairy chocolate buttons for web

Instructions

1. Place a large skillet (or use a griddle), on medium heat over your stovetop. It is very important not to have the skillet too hot. Pancake batter hates a very hot burner. If you are uncertain and want to play it safe go with medium-low heat.
2. Mix the lemon juice and milk in a bowl and let it curdle for about 5 minutes. Once curdled you can begin to add your ingredients.
3. In a large bowl mix, add all wet ingredients with the pumpkin puree to the lemon and milk mixture and mix well.
4. Next, add all dry ingredients. A good tip to follow if you are uncertain about the batter's consistency is, if the batter appears too thin, add a tiny bit more flour. If it appears too thick, add a small amount of almond milk. Depending on what you fancy, here is the rule I follow; the thicker the batter the thicker the pancakes, the thinner the batter the thinner the pancakes.
5. Let the batter rest for a few minutes to allow the baking powder to activate. There's no rushing this so it's best to let it sit.
6. Add some coconut oil to your skillet (or cooking spray), enough to lightly coat the skillet (1/2 tsp. should do you), and pour 1/4 cup of the batter onto the skillet or griddle.
7. Cook the pancakes until bubbles appear in the middle, then it's time to flip.
8. Flip the pancake and cook for 2-3 minutes more. Both sides should be deliciously and evenly cooked.
9. Allow pancakes to completely cool before decorating. You don't want your superb spider webs to run and mesh together.
10. Fill a medium saucepan about halfway with water and bring to a boil. You want to leave enough room in the saucepan to fit a metal or heatproof bowl.
11. Place the non-dairy chocolate buttons in the small heatproof bowl and set them over the boiling water. Stir well and continue to stir occasionally, until the non-dairy chocolate is completely melted.
12. Remove from heat and transfer the nondairy chocolate into a pastry bag. Using your pastry bag decorate your perfect pumpkin pancakes

into the creepiest spider webs your little monster has ever seen! Top with fun spiders for some crawling good fun!

Witch's Notes: For thicker pancakes use 2 ¼ cups flour. For thinner pancakes use 2 cups flour.

PART XV

HAUNTED SPICED OATMEAL

Prep Time: 5 mins / Cook Time: 5-10 mins / Servings: Makes approx. 2

Ingredients

- 1 cup oatmeal
- 2 cup unsweetened vanilla almond milk
- 1-2 tbsp. maple syrup (to taste)
- 1 tbsp. brown sugar (optional)
- ½ tsp. cinnamon
- pinch of nutmeg
- 1 banana
- 1 tbsp. nondairy chocolate sauce
- 1 apricot
- raisons (optional)

Instructions

1. Pour the almond milk into the saucepan and bring it to a boil.
2. Reduce heat to medium-low and add the oats, maple syrup, brown sugar (optional) cinnamon, and nutmeg giving it a good stir. Cook over a low boil for 2-3 minutes.
3. Remove from heat, cover, and let stand for another 2-3 minutes to thicken.
4. Place in a bowl and prepare your boo-tiful bananas (see boo-tiful banana recipe) add the nondairy chocolate sauce to the bottom of the oatmeal. Cut a slice from an apricot and use it as the sun in your bowl. Now you're ready to serve a truly spiced haunted oatmeal that any goblin will want to gobble up!

Witch's Notes: To make the oatmeal thicker add equal amounts of oats to the milk. For the little witch or wizard with a sweet tooth, add 2 tbsp. of maple syrup and 2 tbsp. of brown sugar. Feel free to throw in some raisins for some added flavor and fun!

PART XVI

PERFECTLY PETRIFYING PUMPKIN SOUP

Prep Time: 5-10 mins / Cook Time: 30 mins / Servings: Makes approx. 4

Ingredients

- 2 cups vegetable stock
- 2 cloves of garlic (crushed)
- 1 small white onion (chopped)
- 9 cups pumpkin from 2 small baking pumpkins (peeled and cubed not cooked)
- 1 cup full-fat coconut milk from can
- ¼ tsp. nutmeg
- ½ tsp. thyme
- 1/2 tsp. salt

- 1/4 tsp. ground black pepper
- 1 tbsp. coconut oil

Web

- non-dairy sour cream
- black olives

Instructions

1. Heat the coconut oil in a large pot on medium heat with the chopped onion and garlic. Sautee for about 4 minutes giving it the occasional stir.
2. Add the coconut milk and vegetable stock and stir all the ingredients.
3. Next, add all your spices to the pot.
4. Now for the pumpkin. Add in your cubed pumpkin and continue to cook on medium heat until the soup comes to a low boil. Always give your ingredients a stir here and there. They need your attention.
5. Lower the heat and allow it to simmer for 20-25 minutes. You'll know when it's ready when the pumpkin is delightfully tender.
6. Blender time! Remove from heat and transfer into an electric blender mixing bowl. On medium speed mix together for a good minute. This makes it oh so creamy!
7. Pour into a white soup bowl. I find the color combination with the orange soup and a white bowl to look very appealing!
8. Now for the fun Halloween food art! Scoop nondairy sour cream into a pastry bag. Using your pastry bag decorate your perfect pumpkin soup into a ghastly masterpiece of spidery art! Add a spider to your web with one large black olive as the body. Slice up another black olive using the pieces as legs. Position the sliced legs on either side of the whole black olive. Now you have a creepy-crawly friend!

PART XVII
POLTERGEIST PARTY MASHED POTATOES

Prep Time: 5 mins / Cook Time: 25-30 mins / Servings: Makes approx. 6-8

Ingredients

- 6-8 medium to large Yukon potatoes (any white potato will work)
- 2 tsp sea salt
- ½ tsp. ground black pepper
- ¼ cup unsweetened nondairy milk (I use almond milk)
- 1 tbsp. melted non-dairy butter

Instructions

1. Fill a large pot with water and bring to a boil on high heat.
2. Add potatoes, reduce to medium heat and cook for 12-15 minutes until potatoes are tender and you can pierce them with a fork. No one likes hard mashed potatoes so make sure they are nice and tender.
3. Remove from heat and drain water, add the potatoes to a large mixing

bowl.

4. Mash time! Using a potato masher, give the potatoes a good mash-up!
5. Transfer potatoes to a standalone mixer and mix until they are oh so soft and deliciously creamy looking.
6. Add the nondairy milk nice and slowly. You don't want any splatters flying out of the bowl. You want the consistency to be somewhat firm as you will be placing them in a pastry bag so go slow when adding the milk and keep an eye on the consistency.
7. Add the remaining ingredients and give it one more good monster mash!
8. Allow the potatoes to cool before scooping them into the pastry bag.
9. I use a wide mouth piping tip for this step.
10. Pipe out your ghost onto a serving tray and place two cooked peas as eyes in your ghoulish friends! Don't forget the mouth! Use a toothpick and gently carve a cute smile or boo mouth.

PART XVIII
REVOLTING MEATLESS MEATBALLS

Prep Time: 20 mins / Cook Time: 20-25 mins / Servings: Makes approx. 6-8

Ingredients

- 1 cup chickpeas (drained)
- 1 cup cooked brown rice
- 1 flax egg
- ½ cup breadcrumbs
- 4 cloves garlic (minced)
- 1 cup yellow onion (chopped)
- 1 tsp. marjoram
- 2 tbsp. dried Italian spice blend
- ½ tsp. salt
- ½ tsp. basil
- ¼ tsp. black pepper

- 1 tbsp. non-dairy butter (for greasing the baking sheet)

Instructions

1. Preheat your oven to 400 degrees Fahrenheit.
2. Drain the chickpeas but do not discard the water in the can. You can use it later if your mixture is too dry by adding a tablespoon of chickpea water to the mixture at a time until the consistency is just right!
3. Blend the chickpeas in a stand mixer until all are broken down.
4. Next prepare your flax egg and mix it with the chickpeas.
5. Add all the remaining ingredients to the mixer. If the mixture appears too sticky and isn't able to form a ball, add more breadcrumbs, half a tablespoon at a time. The batter should be easy to roll without cracking.
6. Now the fun part! Time to shape your meatless meatballs! Roll the batter into small balls in between your hands and place them on a lightly greased baking sheet.
7. Bake the meatless meatballs for 20-25 minutes until golden brown. Check on these revolting balls at 20 minutes to make sure they are not burning. Every oven is different, so I always advise that you keep an eye on them.
8. Serve over pasta, or with mashed potatoes.

Witch's Comments: If you have a finicky eater, like one of my ghouls, then you are probably familiar with the frustration of trying to get them to try and eat new things. One trick I use is to have them get involved with the cooking. For this recipe have your little monster roll out the balls and come up with a fun story while you do it. Tell them these are magical Halloween vegan balls and if they don't eat them up, they will roll off the plate, right out the window, and into the neighbor's garden! They know it's not true, but it adds a bit of magic and fun and that's what Halloween cooking is all about.

PART XIX

GRUESOME GOBLIN FETTUCCINE WITH SPECTACULAR SPECTER SAUCE

Prep Time: 5 mins / Cook Time: 8-12 mins / Servings: Makes approx. 2

Ingredients

For The Pasta

- 1 lb. green fettuccine pasta

For The Sauce

- 1 large can crushed tomatoes (28 ounces)

- 1 yellow onion (finely chopped)
- 2 cloves garlic (minced)
- 1 tbsp. extra virgin olive oil
- 1 tsp. dried oregano
- 1 tbsp. Italian seasoning blend
- 1 tsp. basil
- 1 tsp. salt
- 1 tbsp. white sugar
- black olives

For The Eyeballs

To add non-dairy mozzarella eyeballs, use MozzaRisella Vegan Log Cheese (or any non-dairy mozzarella log cheese you have available) and slice in the shape of quarters. Use black olives to place in the center of the sliced mozzarella pieces and use them on top of your sauce to create eyeballs.

Instructions

1. In a medium saucepan bring the water to a boil to cook your fettuccini. While you wait for the water to boil move on to the Spectacular Specter Sauce.
2. In a saucepan warm 1 tablespoon of olive oil over medium-high heat. Add the onions and sauté until softened and translucent, about 2 minutes. Next, add garlic and cook for another minute.
3. Add the tomatoes (including juices from the can), olive oil, salt, and all spices to the saucepan and stir well.
4. Bring the sauce to a simmer over medium-high heat then reduce the temperature and simmer while you prepare your fettuccini. Make sure to give your sauce the occasional stir. This spectacular specter sauce does not like to be ignored.
5. Once the water has boiled for your fettuccini add the pasta and cook until tender. Drain the fettuccini and plate it in a circular pattern. Top with your specter sauce only covering the center of the pasta. You want to see that gruesome green color on the plate. Here is my favorite part! Top the sauce with nondairy edible eyeballs of your choice and watch this goblin pasta truly become gruesome!

Witch's Notes: If you cannot find green pasta there are other variations you can do to this recipe with the same dynamic outcome. Omit the green pasta altogether and just use plain pasta with the red sauce. If you have your heart set on green pasta, alternatively you can swap out the red pasta sauce and use a basil pesto which will turn your pasta green. See the recipe for Ghastly Grim Basil Pesto. Once the pesto is prepared simply mix it with your cooked pasta. This will turn your pasta green but you will have specks of basil on the pasta so it will not be a smooth appearance, however, I personally find it looks rather gruesome and adds to this goblin dish!

PART XX
WICKED EASY WEBBED PIZZA

Prep Time: 15 mins / Cook Time: 15-20 mins / Servings: Makes approx. 2 mediums or 4 smalls

Ingredients

- 1 tsp. instant yeast
- ½ cup warm water
- 1 tbsp. all-purpose flour
- 1 ¼ cup all-purpose flour
- 1/3 tsp. salt
- 1 tbsp. olive oil
- 1 tsp. olive oil (to coat the bowl)
- tomatoes (sliced) optional
- red onion (sliced) optional
- non-dairy mozzarella cheese

- tomato pizza sauce (or refer to Spectacular Specter Sauce if you would like to make your own)
- black olives (optional to make edible spiders)

Instructions

1. Preheat oven to 420 degrees.
2. In a mixing bowl, mix warm water, yeast, and 1 tbsp. all-purpose flour. Let it sit for a couple of minutes to activate the yeast. Make sure the water it's warm and not hot. Hot water kills the yeast.
3. Add 1 cup of all-purpose flour, salt, and olive oil to the mixture and mix well. Slowly add the remaining ¼ cup all-purpose flour and mix thoroughly. If using a stand mixer, mix on slow speed with a bread dough attachment. If the dough is too sticky add an extra tablespoon of flour. The aim is to have the dough slightly sticky but not so sticky that you are unable to form a ball.
4. Rub and coat the inside of a bowl and place the dough inside making sure to rub the tops and bottom of the dough in the oil. Cover with a kitchen towel for about 15 minutes.
5. Once the dough is ready, roll your dough on a lightly floured surface about the size of your pizza pan. For thin-crust divide the dough into two balls and bake on two pizza pans.
6. Place the dough on your pizza pan.
7. Top each pizza with your chosen tomato sauce. Optional toppings to add are sliced tomatoes and sliced red onions. You don't want to add too many toppings or colors to these pizzas because of the spider web theme. Simple is creepier! You want the web to be the main focus in this spider's lair.
8. Use your choice of non-dairy mozzarella cheese and form spider web patterns on the dough.
9. Bake the pizzas for 15 to 20 minutes, until they're golden brown, and the non-dairy cheese is bubbly and melted.
10. Remove the pizzas from the oven and allow them to cool before serving these Wicked Easy Webbed Pizzas to your party guests!

Witch's Notes: Optional step to add edible spiders to the pizza by using black olives. Place one black olive as the body on your pizza and slice up another black olive using the pieces as legs. Position the sliced legs on either side of the whole black olive. Eek! So creepy!

PART XXI

MENACING MONSTER SWEET POTATO BURGER

Prep Time: 15 mins / Cook Time: about 1.5 hours / Servings: Makes approx. 10-12

Ingredients

- 2 large sweet potatoes
- 1 cup black beans (rinsed and drained)
- 1 ½ cups cooked brown rice
- ½ pecan meal (almond meal works too)
- 1 small sweet onion (chopped)
- 1 tsp. garlic powder
- 1 tsp. paprika
- 2 tsp. cumin
- ¼ chipotle powder
- 1 tsp. chili powder

- ½ tsp. salt
- ½ tsp. black pepper

For The Toppings And Monster Face

- 6-8 buns
- green olives
- non-dairy sliced cheddar cheese
- sliced sandwich pickles
- lettuce
- sliced tomatoes
- toothpicks

Instructions

1. Preheat oven to 400 degrees Fahrenheit.
2. Slice the sweet potatoes down the center lengthwise. Rub olive oil on the meat of the sweet potatoes and place the sweet potatoes cut side down on a baking sheet. Roast until tender and you can pierce with a fork, about 30 to 40 minutes.
3. While the sweet potatoes are baking move on to your brown rice. Follow the instructions on your rice bag or box. Add brown rice and water in a saucepan over medium-high heat and bring to a boil. Cover with a lid and simmer on low until rice is fluffy.
4. Once sweet potatoes are done, remove them from the oven and cool completely. Remove the skins and chop the sweet potatoes into cubes.
5. In a stand mixer (or large mixing bowl if you are using an electric mixer) combine the cubed sweet potatoes, black beans, rice, pecan meal, onion, cumin, chili powder, garlic powder, chipotle, paprika, black pepper, and salt.
6. Line a baking sheet with parchment paper.
7. Form mixture into patties and place on parchment paper. Lightly press down on each patty to help with even cooking. Coat the tops with olive oil.
8. Place the baking sheet in the refrigerator for 15-20 to help firm up the patties. This aids in keeping their shape.
9. Bake for about 35 minutes flipping them halfway.
10. Once cooked remove from oven.

11. To turn these sweet potato black bean burgers into menacing monsters, place a patty in a bun. Layer up your toppings starting with a piece of lettuce, a slice of tomato, and a slice of non-dairy cheddar cheese.
12. With kitchen, scissors cut the non-dairy cheese into triangle wedges, so it resembles jagged teeth.
13. Place a sliced pickle vertically on top of the nondairy cheese and add the top of the bun. Half of the pickle should be sticking out of the patty, to resemble a tongue. Stick two green olives on toothpicks and place them on the bun to create eyes.

3. Desserts

- Trick Or Treat Jelly
- Shockingly Simple Sugar Cookies
- Under Your Spell Witch Fingers
- Frightening Frosting
- Cursed Pumpkin Frosting
- Morbid Marshmallow Syrup
- Screaming Pumpkins Sugar Cookies
- Banshee Pumpkin Cupcakes With Wicked Witch Raspberry Syrup
- Going Batty Chocolate Cupcakes
- Eerie Edible Eyeballs
- Wicked Witch Raspberry Syrup
- Vampire Vanilla ice cream
- Spooky Spirit Cake Squares with Morbid Marshmallow Syrup
- Skele-cakes With White Chocolate Pretzels
- Bewitching Autumn Apples
- Chronically Confused Chocolate Chip Cookies
- Spell Binding Candy Apples

PART XXII

TRICK OR TREAT JELLY

Prep Time: 15 mins / Cook Time: 1 hour / Total Time 4 hours / Servings: Makes approx. 5-7

Ingredients

Orange Jelly

- 1 cup orange juice
- 1 cup water
- ¼ cup sugar
- 1 tsp. agar-agar powder

White Jelly

- 1 can coconut milk
- 1 cup water
- ½ tsp. agar-agar powder

- ½ cup sugar

Yellow Jelly

- 1 cup pineapple juice
- 1 cup water
- ¼ cup sugar
- 1 tsp. agar-agar powder

Instructions

1. Start with the orange Jelly. Dissolve the agar-agar powder in the water.
2. In a saucepan over medium heat, combine the orange juice and sugar into the water and the agar-agar powder.
3. Bring the mixture to a boil over medium heat. Stir well and continue to stir occasionally while it boils for about 2 minutes.
4. Remove from the heat pour half of the mixture (you will want to save the other half to top off the cups as the final layer.) into individual cups and let it sit until firm about 15 mins. Keep the other half in a saucepan on low heat, stirring it occasionally. You can pop the dishes in the refrigerator to help the setting process while you move on to your next layer the coconut Jelly.
5. In a saucepan over medium heat, combine the water and agar-agar powder and stir well.
6. Bring to a full boil, continue to stir for about 1 minute. You want the agar-agar powder completely dissolved before moving on to the other ingredients.
7. Add the sugar and stir until dissolved.
8. Next add the coconut milk, giving it a good stir, and remove it from heat.
9. If your orange Jelly is set (if not keep the coconut Jelly on low heat, stirring occasionally) pour the coconut Jelly over top of each orange layer in the cups to create a thin layer. Allow to cool and set, about 15 mins while you move on to the pineapple Jelly.
10. Now prepare the pineapple Jelly.
11. Dissolve the agar-agar powder in the water.
12. In a saucepan over medium heat, combine the pineapple juice and sugar to the water and the agar-agar powder.

13. Bring the mixture to a boil over medium heat. Stir well and continue to stir occasionally while it boils for about 2 minutes.
14. Remove from the heat and pour on top of the coconut layers once they have set.
15. Take the remaining orange Jelly from the saucepan and top all cups as a final layer.
16. Place all cups into the refrigerator and let them set for a least 3 hours. Overnight is best but if you can't wait to serve these spectacular candy corn treats 3 hours will work. Trick or Treat!

Witch's Notes: Optional step, add Edible Eyeballs to give your colorful candy corn Jelly some creative personality! See the recipe for Edible Eyeballs to make your own.

Witch's Comments: Traditional Jell-O is not vegan. Jello-O is made with gelatin which is a protein obtained by boiling skin, tendons, ligaments, and or bones in water. My kids love anything that is made with gelatin, so it was imperative I found an alternative to gelatin. Agar-agar works just like gelatin, but it is completely plant-based derived from seaweed. You will achieve the exact same results using agar-agar powder.

PART XXIII

SHOCKINGLY SIMPLE SUGAR COOKIES

Prep Time: 10 mins / Cook Time: 40-50 mins / Servings: Makes approx. 12-14 depending on your cookie cutter size

Ingredients

- ½ cup non-dairy butter (softened)
- ½ cup sugar
- 1 ½ cups all-purpose flour
- ¼ cup brown sugar
- 1 tsp. vanilla extract
- 1 tsp. baking soda
- 1/4 tsp. salt
- 2 tbsp. non-dairy milk (I use vanilla almond milk, but any non-dairy milk

will work)

- non-dairy frosting (for homemade see index)

Instructions

1. Preheat the oven to 350 degrees Fahrenheit.
2. In a stand mixer, cream the nondairy softened butter and vanilla extract in the mixer.
3. In a medium bowl mix the flour, baking soda, and salt.
4. Add the dry ingredients to the sugar, non-dairy butter, and vanilla extract and mix well. It should be at a crumbly consistency at this point.
5. Next, add the non-dairy milk to the batter to form a ball of dough. If it's too crumbly add a tiny bit more nondairy milk. If it becomes too wet, add a touch of flour. Crumbly batter is better batter with this recipe.
6. Cover your batter with vegan wax wrap (plastic wrap works as well) and place in the freezer for 15 to 30 minutes to firm. This will prevent your cookies from spreading.
7. Flour your work surface and place the ball of dough on your work area.
8. Now roll out your dough to about the size of a cookie sheet, using a rolling pin.
9. Shape time! Once you got your dough spread out, grab your most horrifying and hair-raising cookie cutters and start cutting out your cookies.
10. Line a cookie sheet with parchment paper and place your cookies onto the sheet. Make sure to leave a bit of room in between the cookies for them to expand and spread.
11. Bake in the oven for 10-12 minutes. You can check the centers of the cookies with a toothpick. If it comes out clean, they're done! If it comes out wet, put them back in for another minute or two.
12. Remove from the oven and allow to cool completely on a wired rack before decorating these shockingly simple sugar cookies.

Witch's Notes: This is such a versatile recipe. You can mold shapes from the batter to make witch fingers or cut out shapes using a cookie cutter. To make your own frosting see recipe index.

Witch's Comments: If you have never made homemade frosting before, give it a go! I felt too intimidated to make my own frosting until I discovered just how simple and delicious it is!

PART XXIV

UNDER YOUR SPELL WITCH FINGERS

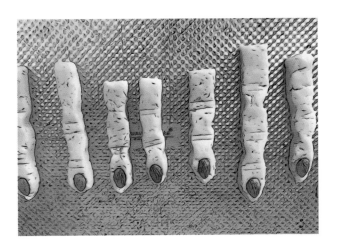

Prep Time: 10 mins / Cook Time: 40-50 mins / Servings: Makes approx. 8-10

Ingredients

- ½ cup non-dairy butter (softened)
- ½ cup sugar
- 1 ½ cups all-purpose flour
- ¼ cup brown sugar
- 1 tsp. vanilla extract
- 1/4 tsp. baking soda
- 1/4 tsp. salt
- 2 tbsp. non-dairy milk (I use vanilla almond milk, but any non-dairy milk will work)
- non-dairy frosting (for homemade see index)
- almonds

Instructions

1. Preheat the oven to 350 degrees Fahrenheit.
2. In a stand mixer, cream the non-dairy softened butter and vanilla extract in the mixer.
3. In a medium bowl mix the flour, baking soda, and salt.
4. Add the dry ingredients to the sugar, nondairy butter, and vanilla extract and mix well. It should be at a crumbly consistency at this point.
5. Next, add the non-dairy milk to the batter to form a ball of dough. If it's too crumbly add a tiny bit more nondairy milk. If it becomes too wet, add a touch of flour. Crumbly batter is the better batter with this recipe.
6. Cover your batter with vegan wax wrap (plastic wrap works as well) and place in the freezer for 15 to 30 minutes to firm. This prevents them from spreading.
7. Flour your work surface and place the ball of dough on your work area.
8. Now roll out your dough to about the size of a cookie sheet, using a rolling pin.
9. Using a pizza cutter, cut the dough into 1″ wide x 4″ long strips.
10. Press almonds in one end of the breadsticks for the fingernails.
11. Pinch the top of each finger (below the almond nail) to look like knuckles, then lightly score each knuckle with a sharp knife. This gives the fingers dimension and texture.
12. Line a cookie sheet with parchment paper and place your cookies onto the sheet. Make sure to leave a bit of room in between the cookies for them to expand and spread.
13. Bake in the oven for 10-12 minutes. You can check the centers of the cookies with a toothpick. If it comes out clean, they're done! If it comes out wet, put them back in for another minute or two.
14. Remove from the oven and allow to cool completely on a wired rack.
15. Optional step, remove the almond (don't worry it will come off easily) and pipe chocolate frosting around and inside the nail bed. Place the almond back on top for a dramatic effect.

Witch's Notes: These beauties look and taste great on their own and do not require any frosting. However, you could add a cup of frosting in a dipping bowl as an option with your spread. These are eye stoppers at any party so display them in a unique way to add more drama to your table. Add spider rings to the fingers as an added treat for the kids. Display them in mason jars, mini cauldrons, or carved-out baking pumpkins. I use just a tad bit of baking soda and omit the baking powder altogether as this is a leavening agent and causes the cookies to spread.

Witch's Comments: One year I grounded up non-dairy chocolate cookies in a food processor and made a bed of dirt with the crumbs. I filled up a small garden pot and placed the witch fingers inside with a few gummy worms sticking out. This was a fun project, but it does require a lot of cookies. Another option is to sprinkle a plate with the cookie dirt and rest the witch fingers on top. Sprinkle each finger with a bit of the cookie dirt for a crackling good time!

PART XXV
FRIGHTENING FROSTING

Prep Time: 10 mins / Cook Time: 10 mins / Servings: Makes 12 (2-tbsp. servings)

Ingredients

- ½ cup non-dairy butter
- 1 cup powdered sugar
- 1 tbsp. vanilla almond milk (regular almond milk works as well or any non-dairy milk)
- 2 tbsp. cornstarch (option to thicken)

Instructions

1. In a mixing bowl whip, the non-dairy butter with a stand mixer on low speed.

2. Add the powdered sugar and vanilla almond milk and mix well.
3. Mix until the consistency is very sticky.
4. You can separate the frosting into 2 bowls to make two different colored frostings or keep it in one bowl for one color. Add a drop of food coloring into each bowl and mix in to create your frightening frosting.
5. I like to place the frosting in the refrigerator to firm and thicken before I use it.

Witch's Notes: To make the frosting chocolate add 3tbsp. of unsweetened cocoa powder.

PART XXVI
CURSED PUMPKIN FROSTING

Prep Time: 10 mins / Cook Time: 10 mins / Servings: Makes 12 (2-tbsp. servings)

Ingredients

- ½ cup dairy-free cream cheese
- ½ cup non-dairy butter
- 2 cups powdered sugar
- 1 tbsp. pumpkin puree
- 1 tsp. vanilla extract
- ½ tsp. pumpkin spice
- 2 tbsp. corn starch (optional to thicken)

Instructions

1. Using a stand mixer, add the nondairy cream cheese, non-dairy butter, and powdered sugar, mix on slow speed.
2. Add the pumpkin puree, vanilla extract, and pumpkin pie spice, blend on slow speed in a stand mixer.
3. Mix until the consistency is very sticky. If it appears too thin you can thicken it up by adding corn starch 1 tbsp. at a time. Optional step, place the frosting in the refrigerator to firm and thicken, before placing it in your pastry bags.
4. You can separate the frosting into 2 bowls to make two different

colored frostings using food coloring. Place in a pastry bag and use it to decorate all your devilish treats!

PART XXVII

MORBID MARSHMALLOW SYRUP

Prep Time: 10 mins / Cook Time: 10 mins / Servings: Makes 12 (2-tbsp. servings)

Ingredients

- ½ cup brine from a can of chickpeas (the water from the can)
- 1 tsp. vanilla extract
- ¾ cup white sugar
- ¼ tsp. cream of tartar

Instructions

1. In a standalone mixer (or whisk by hand) add the chickpea brine, vanilla extract, and cream of tartar and mix on slow speed.
2. Slowly start to add in the sugar and continue to mix at a slow speed.

3. Mix for about 10 minutes until it thickens. You want the consistency to be a thick drizzle.

Witch's Notes: Use with Spooky Spirit Cake Squares.

PART XXVIII

SCREAMING PUMPKIN SUGAR COOKIES

Prep Time: 10 mins / Cook Time: 1 hour / Servings: Makes approx. 22-24

Ingredients

- ¼ cup pumpkin puree
- ½ cup non-dairy butter (softened)
- ½ cup sugar
- ¼ cup brown sugar
- 1 ½ cups all-purpose flour
- ½ tbsp. cornstarch
- 1 tsp. baking powder
- ½ tsp. baking soda
- ¼ tsp. salt
- 1 tsp. pumpkin pie spice
- ½ tsp. cinnamon

- 1 tsp. vanilla extract
- 1 tbsp. vanilla almond milk (regular almond milk will work as well)
- non-dairy frosting (for homemade see index)

Instructions

1. Preheat your oven to 350 degrees Fahrenheit.
2. Add softened non-dairy butter, sugar, and vanilla extract to a large mixing bowl and cream with a stand mixer on slow.
3. Add in the brown sugar, pumpkin puree, and beat for 1 minute.
4. Next, add all the dry ingredients to your mixer and mix for 1-2 minutes on slow.
5. Now add the vanilla almond milk and mix until a soft dough is formed. If it appears too wet, add a bit more flour until it becomes thicker and more manageable to form into a ball.
6. Transfer your batter into the freezer, covering it with vegan wax wrap (or plastic wrap), and leave it in for 15-30 minutes to firm.
7. When the batter is ready using an ice-cream scooper, scoop out the chilled dough and roll the batter into balls. (Optional step, carefully flatten the balls with a spoon to help them cook evenly.)
8. Arrange cookies on a clean baking sheet making sure to leave a bit of space in between each cookie for them to expand and spread.
9. Bake in the oven for 10-12 minutes. You can check the centers of the cookies with a toothpick. If it comes out clean, they're done! If it comes out wet, put them back in for another minute or two.
10. Remove from oven and allow to cool on a wired rack, before you frost these Screaming Pumpkin Sugar Cookies and serve them to your eager party guests!

PART XXIX

BANSHEE PUMPKIN CUPCAKES WITH WICKED WITCH SYRUP

Prep Time: 15 mins / Cook Time: 40 mins / Servings: Makes 12

Ingredients

- 2 ¼ cups all-purpose flour
- ½ cup pumpkin puree
- 1 cup white sugar
- ½ cup brown sugar
- 1 ½ tsp. baking powder
- ½ tsp. baking soda
- ½ tsp. salt
- 1 ½ cups vanilla almond milk (any non-dairy milk will work)
- ½ cup walnut oil (any type of vegetable works)
- 1 ½ tsp. vanilla extract
- 1 ½ tsp. pumpkin pie spice

- ½ tsp. cinnamon

Bloody Sauce

- ½ cup fresh raspberries (frozen would work as well)
- ½ cup sugar

Instructions

1. Preheat oven to 350 degrees Fahrenheit.
2. Using a stand mixer cream together the butter, brown sugar, and white sugar in a mixing bowl on slow speed. If mixing by hand whisk briskly.
3. In a mixing bowl mix the pumpkin puree, non-dairy milk, walnut oil, and vanilla extract and mix well.
4. Add the baking powder, baking soda, pumpkin spice, flour, salt and mix well.
5. Add the ingredients to the creamed sugar and mix on slow speed with a stand mixer until smooth (if mixing by hand, mix until all clumps are out).
6. Pour the batter into a spouted cup or jug and pour evenly into the 12 cupcake liners, filling them up about half of the way.
7. Place into the oven and bake for about 15-20 minutes. Test with a toothpick to see if they are ready. If the toothpick comes out clean, they are done.
8. Remove from pan and let cool completely on a wire rack before frosting.
9. While the cupcakes are cooling start to make the raspberry sauce. Yummy!
10. Wash then slice your raspberries (frozen raspberries will work too).
11. Place raspberry slices and sugar in a small saucepan over medium heat. Give them a good mash with a potato masher to get all the delicious juices flowing.
12. Stir occasionally for about 10 minutes.
13. Remove raspberry sauce from heat and allow it to cool so it is not piping hot.
14. Place a cheesecloth into your colander and drain the sauce into a bowl. This eliminates pulps and seeds.
15. Drizzle the raspberry sauce over your cupcakes.

16. Using a toothpick insert one end into a nondairy marshmallow and place the toothpick in the center of your cupcake. Draw a spooky face on the nondairy marshmallow with edible markers.

PART XXX

GOING BATTY CHOCOLATE CUPCAKES WITH CRYPTIC CHOCOLATE FROSTING

Prep Time: 15 mins / Cook Time: 15-20 mins / Servings: Makes 12

Ingredients

For The Cupcakes

- 1 cup sugar
- ½ cup brown sugar
- 1 cup water
- 1/3 cup walnut oil
- 1 tbsp. apple cider vinegar
- 1 tsp. baking soda
- ½ tsp. salt

- 1 tsp. vanilla extract
- ¼ cup unsweetened cocoa powder
- 2 cups all-purpose flour

For Cryptic Chocolate Frosting

- 3 tbsp. nondairy butter
- 1 cup powdered sugar
- ½ cup unsweetened cocoa powder
- 2 tbsp. vanilla almond milk (unsweetened works too)
- 1 tsp. vanilla extract

For The Decorations

- non-dairy Oreo cookies
- non-dairy edible eyeballs (store-bought or see Eerie Eyeball recipe to make your own)

Instructions

1. Preheat the oven to 350 degrees Fahrenheit. Line all your cupcake trays with your favorite Halloween cupcake liners. There are so many cute options to choose from!
2. Mix the flour and cocoa powder into a mixing bowl (or a stand mixer on low speed) and add the baking soda, salt, white and brown sugar, mixing well.
3. Next add the walnut oil, vanilla extract, water, and apple cider vinegar. Mix well, until there are no clumps. If you are mixing by hand use a hand whisker to really smooth up the batter.
4. Transfer the batter into a spouted cup or jug and divide the batter evenly by pouring batter into each cupcake liner, about halfway full.
5. Place the cupcakes into the oven and bake for 15-20 minutes. You know when they are done by inserting a toothpick into the center of one of the cupcakes and it comes out clean.
6. Remove the tray from the oven and let cool. Remove from the pan and let it cool completely on a wire rack before frosting. While the cupcakes are cooling start your Cryptic Chocolate Frosting.
7. Use a stand mixer for your frosting. In a mixing bowl add the non-dairy

butter, powdered sugar, cocoa powder, and vanilla extract, mix well on slow speed. Gradually increase the speed and add the nondairy milk. Mix for another minute until you reached your desired consistency. It should look gloriously creamy!

8. Transfer the frosting into a piping bag. When your cupcakes are cooled, pipe on the frosting gradually working the piping into a peak at the top of each cupcake.

9. Cut the non-dairy Oreos in half and stick on either side of the cupcake to make ears.

10. Use a non-dairy edible eyeball in the center to give your batty cupcakes a personality that will send them flying off your plate!

Witch's Notes: For edible eyeballs use nondairy store-bought or make your own with the Eerie Edible Eyeball recipe.

PART XXXI

EERIE EDIBLE EYEBALLS

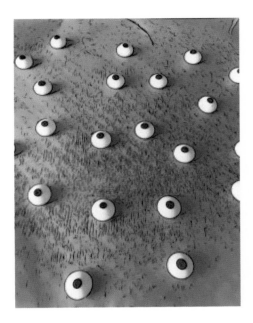

Prep Time: 30 mins / Cook Time: 30 mins / Servings: Makes approx. 120

Ingredients

- 1/3 cup brine from a can of chickpeas (the water inside the can)
- 4 cup powdered sugar
- 1 tsp. cream of tartar
- non-dairy chocolate buttons (non-dairy chocolate chips work too)
- food coloring (optional step)

Instructions

1. In a stand mixer add the chickpea brine and half of the powdered sugar (2 cups) on high speed.
2. Once mixed add the remaining 2 cups of powdered sugar and cream of

tartar.

3. Continue to mix on high speed until peaks have formed and you reached your desired consistency.
4. Remove from the mixer and divide into a pastry bag with a #2 tip for the pupil (to make larger eyes).
5. Lay parchment paper on a cookie sheet.
6. Using your pastry bag pipe out dots on the parchment paper.
7. After you have made rows of eyes top each one with a non-dairy chocolate button or chip.
8. Allow the eyes to air dry for 24 hours to harden and firm. All eyes are on you right now!
9. If you want to use frosting for the iris and not non-dairy chocolate buttons, simply divide your frosting and add black food coloring to one bowl. Place in a pastry bag and pipe the black irises on top of the white pupils (use a tip size smaller than the one you used to make the pupil).

Witch's Notes: Optional step, you can change the iris color and make these eyeballs truly eerie by dividing the royal icing into two bowls and use food coloring on one of the batches to change the iris' color. Then place the royal icing into two separate pastry bags and follow the steps above by piping out the food color iris on top of the white pupils.

Witch's Comments: This recipe can also be used on its own as royal icing (add food color and place in pastry bags). Royal icing is thicker and hardens, so you can get truly creative with it and use it on all your nightmarish decadent desserts from this cookbook.

PART XXXII

WICKED WITCH SYRUP

Prep Time: 10 mins / Cook Time: 10 mins / Servings: Makes 12 (2-tbsp. servings)

Ingredients

- ½ cup raspberries
- ½ cup sugar

Instructions

1. Wash then slice your raspberries (frozen raspberries will work too).
2. Place raspberry slices and sugar in a small saucepan over medium heat. Give them a mash with a potato masher to get all the delicious juices flowing.
3. Stir occasionally for about 10 minutes.

4. Remove the raspberry sauce from heat and allow it to cool so it is not piping hot.
5. Place a cheesecloth into your colander and drain the sauce into a bowl. This eliminates pulps and seeds.
6. Use for cakes, cookies, ice cream, and more.

PART XXXIII

VAMPIRE VANILLA ICE CREAM

Prep Time: 30 mins / Cook Time: 3-4 hours / Servings: Makes 10

Ingredients

- 1 (14oz) can of full-fat coconut milk (chilled in the refrigerator overnight)
- 2 cups raw cashews (unsalted)
- 1 tsp. lemon juice
- 1 tsp. vanilla extract
- ½ cup powdered sugar

Instructions

1. Place the coconut can in the refrigerator overnight.
2. Fill a medium saucepan with water and bring to a boil. Add the cashews and boil for 30 minutes, then drain and discard the water. This makes the cashews soft and easy to blend.

3. In an electric mixer combine your cashews and the meat from the coconut can. You DO NOT want to use the water in the coconut can, only the meat. This is very important.
4. Mix all ingredients together on high speed.
5. Transfer into a bread pan place the pan in the freezer for 3-4 hours until firm. It should now be the right consistency for ice cream.
6. Once it's ready, scoop out your Vampire Vanilla Ice-scream and serve with Bloody Strawberry Sauce.

Witch's Notes: Add a sugar cone on top of your ice-cream scoops and use Eerie Edible Eyeballs to transform it into a witch. Stick pieces of licorice inside the cone so they stick out like hair.

PART XXXIV

SPOOKY SPIRIT CAKE SQUARES WITH MORBID MARSHMALLOW SYRUP

Prep Time: 10 mins / Cook Time: 25-30 mins / Servings: Makes 12

Ingredients

Cake

- 1 cup sugar
- ½ cup brown sugar
- 1 cup water
- 1/3 cup walnut oil
- 1 cup water
- 1 tbsp. apple cider vinegar
- 1 tsp. baking soda

- ½ tsp. salt
- 1 tsp. vanilla extract
- ¼ cup unsweetened cocoa powder
- 2 cups all-purpose flour

Marshmallow Sauce

- ½ cup brine from a can of chickpeas (the water from the can)
- 1 tsp. vanilla extract
- ¾ cup white sugar
- ¼ tsp. cream of tartar

Instructions

1. Preheat the oven to 350 degrees Fahrenheit.
2. In a mixing bowl, mix together all dry ingredients and whisk by hand.
3. In another mixing bowl, mix together all wet ingredients.
4. Combine the wet ingredients with the dry ingredients and mix well until it becomes a smooth batter without lumps. If using a stand mixer, mix on slow to medium speed until all the lumps are gone.
5. Pour the batter into a lightly greased 8-inch square dish and bake at 350 degrees for about 25-30 minutes, or until a toothpick inserted in the middle comes out clean.
6. Place on a wire rack and allow to cool completely.
7. Once cooled, flip the cake out and cut it into squares.
8. Now prepare your non-dairy marshmallow topping.
9. In a stand mixer (or whisk by hand) add the chickpea brine, vanilla, and cream of tartar and mix on slow speed.
10. Slowly start to add in the sugar and continue to mix at a slow speed.
11. Mix for about 10 minutes until it thickens. You want the consistency to be a thick drizzle.
12. Drizzle over your Spooky Spirit Cake Squares and top each with 1 non-dairy marshmallow. Draw faces on your nondairy marshmallows with food coloring pens to make this spirit cake truly come alive!

PART XXXV

SKELE-CAKES WITH WHITE CHOCOLATE PRETZELS

Prep Time: 15-20 mins / Cook Time: 40 mins / Servings: Makes 12

Ingredients

For The Cupcakes

- 2 ¼ cups all-purpose flour
- 1 ½ tsp. baking powder
- ½ tsp. baking soda
- pinch of salt
- 1 ½ cups vanilla almond milk (any non-dairy milk will work)
- 1 cup white sugar
- ½ cup brown sugar
- 2 tsp. vanilla
- ½ cup walnut oil (any vegetable oil will do)

- non-dairy marshmallows

For The Non-dairy White Chocolate Covered Pretzels

- 1 bag mini pretzels
- 1 bag non-dairy white chocolate buttons
- white candy sticks

For The Frosting

- 3 tbsp. nondairy butter
- 1 cup powdered sugar
- 2 tbsp. vanilla almond milk (unsweetened works too)
- 1 tsp. vanilla extract

Instructions

1. Preheat the oven to 350 degrees Fahrenheit and line a cupcake tray with 12 cupcake liners.
2. Using a stand mixer cream together the non-dairy butter, brown sugar, and white sugar in a mixing bowl on slow speed. If mixing by hand whisk briskly.
3. In a mixing bowl mix the non-dairy milk, walnut oil, and vanilla extract and mix well.
4. Add the baking powder, baking soda, flour, salt, and mix well.
5. Add the ingredients to the creamed sugar and mix on slow speed with a stand mixer until smooth. (If mixing by hand, mix until all the lumps are out)
6. Pour the batter into a spouted cup or jug and pour evenly into the 12 cupcake liners, filling them up about half of the way.
7. Place into the oven and bake for about 15-20 minutes. Test with a toothpick to see if they are ready. If the toothpick comes out clean, they are done.
8. Remove from pan and let cool completely on a wire rack before frosting.
9. While your cupcakes are baking move on to your non-dairy white chocolate-covered pretzels.
10. Line a baking sheet with parchment and set it aside.

11. Fill a medium saucepan about halfway with water and bring to a boil. You want to leave enough room in the saucepan to fit a metal or heatproof bowl.

12. Place the non-dairy white chocolate buttons in the small heatproof bowl and set them over the boiling water. Stir well and continue to stir occasionally, until the white non-dairy chocolate is completely melted.

13. Dip each pretzel into the non-dairy white chocolate, rotating it until it is completely coated.

14. Place all dipped pretzels on your parchment-lined baking sheet, and place in the refrigerator for 20 mins or until hardened.

15. By this point, your cupcakes should be done and cooling.

16. Prepare your frosting (see recipe for instructions) or use nondairy store-bought and divide into two bowls. Use black food coloring for one bowl to obtain a grayish-black color. Start with 1 drop of food coloring and add accordingly until you reached your desired shade of black. Keep the other half of the frosting white.

17. Scoop frosting into pastry bags and using a #2 tip, pipe your frosting in two layers on top of each cupcake, starting with white frosting then black frosting.

18. Place a white candy stick in the center of each cupcake.

19. Stack the non-dairy white chocolate pretzels on the candy stick to create skeleton ribs. Top with a nondairy marshmallow. Break a pretzel and use two pieces as arms. Draw a menacing face on your marshmallow using a food coloring pen and serve these scary skeletons at your next party!

Witch's Comments: My daughter loves these cakes and came up with the name Skele-Cakes when baking them. I loved it so much, it stuck! So now that's what we call them. Happy Halloween!

PART XXXVI

BEWITCHING AUTUMN APPLES

Prep Time: 10 mins / Cook Time: 20 mins / Servings: Makes 4

Ingredients

Caramel Sauce

- 1 cup brown sugar
- 1/8 tsp. cream of tartar
- 3 tbsp. coconut milk (the meat from a can)
- 2 tbsp. water
- 1 tsp. vanilla extract

For The Caramel Apples

- 4 apples (I use Granny Smith but any type will do)
- 4 popsicle sticks or twigs

Instructions

1. In a saucepan over low heat, add all ingredients and stir well. Once the coconut milk has melted turn the heat to medium-high.
2. Stir constantly until the mixture reaches a steady boil. Continue to stir on medium-high heat for 1 minute.
3. Reduce heat to low and stir for 2 more minutes.
4. Remove from heat and allow to cool for about 5 minutes until it firms up slightly and has a sticky consistency.
5. While the caramel is cooking, prep your apples. Wash and dry your apples making sure to remove the stems.
6. Line a cookie sheet with parchment paper.
7. Place a popsicle stick or twig inside the tops of your apples. I love the effect of adding twigs as the stem!
8. Dip and roll your apples into the caramel sauce and place on parchment paper. You can use a spoon to help coat the apples starting from the top.

Witch's Notes: Add nuts, candy, or Eerie Edible Eyeballs to your caramel apples for a truly bewitching effect!

PART XXXVII

CHRONICALLY CONFUSED CHOCOLATE CHIP COOKIES

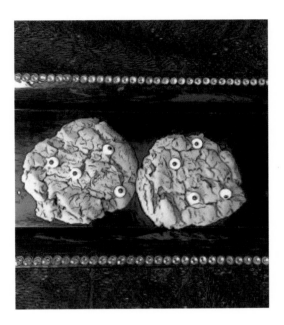

Prep Time: 20 mins / Cook Time: 11-14 mins / Servings: Makes 12

Ingredients

- 2/3 cup non-dairy butter (soften)
- 2 1/2 cups all-purpose flour
- 2/3 cup brown sugar
- 2/3 cup sugar
- 1/3 cup almond milk (any non-dairy milk will do)
- 2 tsp. vanilla extract
- ½ tsp. salt
- 1 tsp. baking soda
- 1 tsp. baking powder

- 1 ½ cups non-dairy chocolate chunks or chips
- non-dairy edible eyeballs (see Eerie Edible Eyeball recipe in index to make your own)

Instructions

1. Preheat oven to 350 degrees Fahrenheit.
2. In a bowl add sugar and soften non-dairy butter and blend well in a stand mixer on low speed (if mixing by hand mix until no lumps remain.)
3. Add all the remaining dry ingredients and mix well.
4. Add the non-dairy milk and vanilla extract and mix one final time.
5. Form dough into a ball and place in the refrigerator for 15-20 mins to firm.
6. Form dough balls, and place on a greased baking tray. Optional step, use a spoon to gently pat down the tops of each dough ball to help with a level shape.
7. Bake for 11-14 minutes.
8. Remove from oven and press Eerie Edible Eyeballs into the cookies. Get imaginative here and mix up your cookie faces! Have one eyeball slightly larger than the other. Use as many or as few eyeballs as you like for these cookies. Having a bit of variety really makes guests take a second look!

Witch's Notes: Smear the chocolate chunks as soon as the cookies come out to make them look distraught and untidy, giving the illusion of a monster mouth.

PART XXXVIII

SPELL BINDING CANDY APPLES

Prep Time: 20 mins / Cook Time: 30 mins / Servings: Makes 6

Ingredients

- 6 apples (I use Granny Smith, but any type will do)
- 2 cups sugar
- ¾ cups water
- ½ cup light corn syrup
- ½ tsp. cinnamon
- ½ tsp. vanilla extract (optional)
- ½ tsp pumpkin spice (optional)
- ½ tsp. red food coloring
- 6 popsicle sticks, candy sticks or twigs
- candy thermometer

Instructions

1. Line a baking sheet with parchment paper and spray it generously with coconut oil cooking spray (any cooking spray will work). Sprinkle the sheet with brown sugar and set it aside.
2. In a heavy-bottomed saucepan mix together the water, sugar, corn

syrup, and food coloring. You should have a gorgeous red color in your pan!

3. Bring your mixture to a boil and continue to boil and bubble until it reaches 300 degrees. Using a candy thermometer, place the tip in the mixture to check the temperature, but make sure the tip is not touching the bottom of the pot. Stir occasionally as you keep your eye on the mixture. Think of this as your witch's cauldron as you carefully monitor your candy. "Fire burn and cauldron bubble"

4. While the candy mixture is bubbling prepare your apples. Wash and dry all apples. Remove the stems and pierce the top with a popsicle stick, candy stick, or twig.

5. Once the candy mixture has reached 300 degrees, remove the saucepan from the heat and stir in the cinnamon, vanilla extract, and pumpkin spice.

6. Be very careful when dipping your apples into the mixture, it is wickedly hot! The mixture will hard rather rapidly, so work quickly but, cautiously. Holding the stick, dip the apples one at a time, into the candy and roll around the pot to coat evenly.

7. Place apples on the parchment paper to set and firm for about 20-30 minutes.

Witch's Notes: The brown sugar at the bottom gives these candy apples a lovely texture and a bit of a crunch when you bite in! Plus, it just looks positively spell-binding.

Witch's Comments: I had a reader inform me that corn syrup was not available in the UK. If you do not have corn syrup available in your country you can make it using water, sugar, and cream of tartar.

4. Drinks

- Witches' Brew Hot Chocolate
- Wild Wizard Potion
- Zombie Party Punch
- Hobgoblin Pumpkin Punch

PART XXXIX

WITCH'S BREW HOT CHOCOLATE

Prep Time: 1 min / Total Time: 4-5 mins / Servings 1

Ingredients

- 1 cup unsweetened non-dairy milk (I use oat milk, but almond milk will work)
- 1/3 cup coconut milk (from a can)
- 2 tbsp. sugar
- 1 tbsp. non-dairy unsweetened cocoa powder
- 1 tbsp. non-dairy semisweet chocolate chips
- ½ tsp. vanilla extract
- non-dairy marshmallows (optional)
- non-dairy cool whip (optional)

Instructions

1. Add the non-dairy milk and coconut milk to a small saucepan over medium heat. Make sure it doesn't get too hot. You don't want the milk to burn.
2. Whisk together the non-dairy cocoa powder and white sugar in a small bowl.
3. Add the non-dairy cocoa powder and white sugar in the saucepan with the milk and whisk all ingredients together. Work out any lumps.
4. Once it's warm, and all lumps have been whisked out, add the non-dairy chocolate chips and continue to whisk until melted. Look at that chocolate melt! I'm in heaven!
5. Bring to a simmer and add the vanilla extract. Give it one final whisk and remove it from heat.
6. Pour into a witchy Halloween mug and top this decadent drink with non-dairy marshmallows.

Witch's Notes: You can get so decadent with this drink! Use non-dairy cool whip to top your hot chocolate then add gummy worms or eyeballs. Load it up, add a colorful straw and celebrate the season with Witch's Brew Hot Chocolate!

PART XL
WILD WIZARD POTION

Prep Time: 1 min / Total Time: 4-5 mins / Servings 6-8

Ingredients

- 1-liter lemon-lime soda chilled
- 1-liter orange Fanta chilled
- ¼ cup pineapple juice chilled
- non-dairy ice cream (see recipe for Vampire Vanilla ice cream)
- gummy worms (optional) or Eerie Edible Eyeballs (see recipe index)

Instructions

1. Combine the chilled lime soda, orange Fanta and pineapple juice in a large punchbowl. You want the soda nice and cold. No one likes a warm punch.
2. Stir well and top with Vampire Vanilla Ice-Cream. Place gummy worms or Eerie Edible Eyeballs on top of the ice cream to give this potion a

punch that will make your guests say "wow!"

PART XLI

ZOMBIE PARTY PUNCH

Prep Time: 1 min / Total Time: 4-5 mins / Servings 6-8

Ingredients

- 1-liter Sprite (chilled)
- ¼ cup pineapple juice (chilled)
- 4 cups Hawaiian punch green berry rush (chilled)
- non-dairy vanilla ice cream (optional)
- gummy worms (optional)

Instructions

1. Combine the chilled Sprite, Hawaiian punch, and pineapple juice in a large punchbowl. You want the soda nice and cold. Warm punch is too ghoulish for this party.
2. Stir well.
3. Add a scoop of non-dairy ice cream (see Vampire Vanilla Ice Cream

recipe for homemade) before serving. Your guests will be eager to give this punch a go!

4. Top this wicked punch with gummy worms and serve in a mason jar or decorative glass.

PART XLII

HOBGOBLIN PUMPKIN PUNCH

Prep Time: 5 min / Total Time: 4-5 mins / Servings 4

Ingredients

- 1 cup orange juice (chilled)
- 1 cup water (cold)
- 1 cup apple juice(chilled)
- 1 cup pineapple juice (chilled)
- ¼ tsp. grated ginger
- ¼ tsp. allspice
- ¼ tsp. cinnamon
- 1tbsp. brown sugar
- ½ cup pumpkin puree (not pie filling)
- 1 cup of ice
- 4 small pumpkins or punchbowl

Instructions

1. Place pumpkin puree, spices, and ice in a blender and blend.
2. Add, orange juice, apple juice, pineapple juice, and water. Stir it all together.

3. Carve out the top of your small pumpkins and clean out the insides, removing all seeds and pulp. Save seeds to roast as a delicious snack and discard the pulp.
4. Fill each pumpkin with punch and place the top back on. Glue googly eyeballs on your pumpkins and add a decorative straw. Refrigerate until ready to use.

Witch's Notes: You can get crazy creative with your pumpkins by adding witches' hats to the tops, or stencil bewitching designs, such as bats, cats, and Halloween ghouls. Don't be afraid to tap into your witchy vibes and try new things like stenciling a crescent moon or gluing on stars.

Witch's Comments: For one of our Halloween parties we had each child go to the pumpkin patch (I made one in the garden with hay stalks and small pumpkins) and choose a pumpkin. With adult supervision, we helped them carve out the top of their pumpkins and scoop out the insides. We supplied the kids with decorations to use on their pumpkins such as glitter, rhinestones, foam stickers, eyes, eyepatches, washable paints, and markers to draw faces. Once all the pumpkins were decorated, we filled each one with their choice of punch. Throw in a decorative straw and you got a party favorite on your hands! Everything is more fun (and tastes better) for kids when they get to be involved.

Thank you to my editor Fallak Tabassum, for her attention to detail and time devoted to *A Very Vegan Halloween*. And for also being my recipe tester and going the extra mile!

A massive thank you to all my friends and family for their support, encouragement, and eagerness to try the recipes in *A Very Vegan Halloween: The Witches' Cauldron Cookbook*.

To my ultimate taste testers; Penelope, Jude, and Dave. Thank you for always having room for one more bite and one more recipe! This witch loves her hungry, happy ghouls!

About The Author

Rebecca Henry is a world traveler living abroad in England. Besides being an American author of her two vegan cookbooks, Rebecca is also an author of fiction.

Rebecca is a vegan, gardener, wife, and mom, who practices yoga. Her favorite season is autumn and her favorite holiday is Halloween, with a passion for anything witchy! Rebecca began cooking and baking when she became a vegan in 2014.